MY FATHER'S LIFE

Dad, I want to know
everything about you.

chartwell
books

FATHER, TELL ME YOUR STORY

Dad, I adore you. From the very first moment I saw your face beaming down upon me with unconditional love, I've felt protected and safe. Your smile was my first sunshine, and I've flourished as a result of its radiance.

Throughout my life you've been there to give me support, encouragement, and —when I need it most —a swift kick in the rear. You're both my toughest critic and my biggest fan, and I appreciate that you challenge me to be the very best version of myself that I can be.

In some ways, I feel like I know you so well. I'm an expert at reading the most subtle change of expression on your face. I know exactly what topics to bring up when I want to provoke you and I can always tell before anyone else when you're about to laugh. But what I'd like to learn more about is how you became the amazing man you are today.

I'm curious about it all —the people, the experiences, and the things that played a part in shaping you into the man I know and the dad I love.

I want to know all about the person you were and the life you had long before I came into the picture. I'm asking you to take your time and answer each of the questions in this journal as thoughtfully and thoroughly as possible. Share all of your stories with me: the happy ones, the sad ones, the good ones, the bad ones. No detail is too dull or too small, I want to know anything and everything.

Father, please, tell me your story.

CHAPTER I

EARLY CHILDHOOD & HERITAGE

A bright shaft of sunlight falling across the ceiling, birds singing outside an open window, feeling cozy while swaddled in a freshly laundered blanket.

"THE HEART OF A FATHER IS THE MASTERPIECE OF NATURE." —Abbe Prevost

What is your birthday and what time of day were you born? Where were you born?

_____

_____

_____

_____

_____

_____

_____

_____

_____

_____

_____

_____

_____

_____

_____

_____

_____

_____

_____

_____

_____

_____

_____

_____

_____

_____

"IN THAT BOOK WHICH IS MY MEMORY, ON THE FIRST PAGE OF THE CHAPTER THAT IS THE DAY WHEN I FIRST MET YOU, APPEAR THE WORDS, 'HERE BEGINS A NEW LIFE.'" —Dante

Are there any stories about your birth that were told to you by your parents or other family members?

What is your full name and what is the story behind it, were you named after someone? What about your middle name?

What is your mother's full name and when and where was she born?

_____
_____
_____
_____
_____
_____
_____
_____
_____
_____
_____
_____
_____
_____
_____
_____
_____
_____
_____
_____
_____
_____
_____
_____
_____
_____
_____

"LET THY CHILD'S FIRST LESSON BE OBEDIENCE, AND THE SECOND WILL BE WHAT
THOU WILT." —Benjamin Franklin.

What is your father's full name and when and where was he born?

_____
_____
_____
_____
_____
_____
_____
_____
_____
_____
_____
_____
_____
_____
_____
_____
_____
_____
_____
_____
_____
_____
_____
_____
_____
_____
_____
_____
_____

"A FATHER IS NEITHER AN ANCHOR TO HOLD US BACK, NOR A SAIL TO TAKE US THERE, BUT A GUIDING LIGHT WHOSE LOVE SHOWS US THE WAY." —Unknown

How did your parents meet and what were their ages when they got married?

Describe your father. What type of work did he do for a living? What were his hobbies?

Describe your mother. What did she do for a living? What were her hobbies?

_____

_____

_____

_____

_____

_____

_____

_____

_____

_____

_____

_____

_____

_____

_____

_____

_____

_____

_____

_____

_____

_____

_____

_____

_____

_____

"FATHER! —TO GOD HIMSELF WE CANNOT GIVE A HOLIER NAME."
—William Wordsworth

Describe your maternal grandparents and the relationship you had with them.

"MY FATHER WAS A FARMER UPON THE CARRICK BORDER, O,
AND CAREFULLY HE BRED ME IN DECENCY AND ORDER, O..." —Robert Burns

Describe your paternal grandparents and the relationship you had with them.

How much time did you spend with extended family growing up?

Tell me about your brothers and sisters —their names, birthdays, and a few
adjectives to best describe each.

"THE CHILD IS FATHER OF THE MAN." —William Wordsworth

Using all five senses, describe your earliest memory in as much detail as possible.

"IT IS FAMILIARITY WITH LIFE THAT MAKES TIME SPEED QUICKLY. WHEN EVERY DAY IS A STEP IN THE UNKNOWN, AS FOR CHILDREN, THE DAYS ARE LONG WITH GATHERING OF EXPERIENCE." —George Gissing

What was the first word your parents say that you spoke out loud and what is the story behind it?

What do you remember about your parents putting you to bed?

What books and songs do you remember your parents or other family members reading and singing to you?

_____

_____

_____

_____

_____

_____

_____

_____

_____

_____

_____

_____

_____

_____

_____

_____

_____

_____

_____

_____

_____

_____

_____

_____

_____

_____

_____

"SPARE THE ROD AND SPOIL THE CHILD —THAT IS TRUE. BUT, BESIDE THE ROD, KEEP AN APPLE TO GIVE HIM WHEN HE HAS DONE WELL." —Martin Luther

Describe the sight, feel, and smell of the first stuffed animal you remember having.

_____

_____

_____

_____

_____

_____

_____

_____

_____

_____

_____

_____

_____

_____

_____

_____

_____

_____

_____

_____

_____

_____

_____

_____

_____

"IF BY CHANCE I TALK A LITTLE WILD, FORGIVE ME; I HAD IT FROM
MY FATHER." —William Shakespeare

Is there anything you remember not liking at all when you were very little, such as an object or an activity?

What was your most cherished possession that you recall from this time in your life and what is the story behind it?

Are there any stories you remember your parents telling you about what you were like as an infant?

_____

_____

_____

_____

_____

_____

_____

_____

_____

_____

_____

_____

_____

_____

_____

_____

_____

_____

_____

_____

_____

_____

_____

_____

"MEMORY IS THE DIARY WE ALL CARRY ABOUT WITH US." —Oscar Wilde

CHAPTER II

CHILDHOOD

The tickle of grass on your face as you roll down
a hill, the sharp sting of antiseptic poured over a
scraped knee, ice cream on a hot summer's day.

"THE STREETS LOOKED SMALL, OF COURSE. THE STREETS THAT
WE HAVE ONLY SEEN AS CHILDREN ALWAYS DO I BELIEVE
WHEN WE GO BACK TO THEM." —Charles Dickens

What toys do you remember playing with most as a child?

When you were little, what did you want to be when you grew up and where did that idea come from?

_____

_____

_____

_____

_____

_____

_____

_____

_____

_____

_____

_____

_____

_____

_____

_____

_____

_____

_____

_____

_____

_____

_____

_____

_____

_____

"MY FATHER KNOWS THE PROPER WAY THE NATION SHOULD BE RUN; HE TELLS US CHILDREN EVERY DAY JUST WHAT SHOULD NOW BE DONE." —Edgar Guest

What was your most favorite game to play when you were playing with friends?

"SO WAS I ONCE MYSELF A SWINGER OF BIRCHES. AND SO I DREAM OF GOING
BACK TO BE." —Robert Frost

Describe your childhood bedroom and list five objects that you remember most vividly.

What was your neighborhood like growing up and what do you remember about your neighbors?

What were a few of your favorite foods when you were little?

"THE WORDS THAT A FATHER SPEAKS TO HIS CHILDREN IN THE PRIVACY OF HOME ARE NOT HEARD BY THE WORLD, BUT, AS IN WHISPERING-GALLERIES, THEY ARE CLEARLY HEARD AT THE END AND BY POSTERITY." —Jean Paul Richter

35

Tell me the names of any pets you had and a little bit about each one of them.

_____

_____

_____

_____

_____

_____

_____

_____

_____

_____

_____

_____

_____

_____

_____

_____

_____

_____

_____

_____

_____

_____

_____

_____

_____

"ALL THE LEARNIN' MY FATHER PAID FOR WAS A BIT O' BIRCH AT ONE END AND AN ALPHABET AT THE OTHER." —George Eliot

What cartoons do you remember watching and loving the most?

What were some of your childhood nicknames and were there any that you did not like?

Did your neighborhood or school have a bully when you were little and did they ever target you?

_____

_____

_____

_____

_____

_____

_____

_____

_____

_____

_____

_____

_____

_____

_____

_____

_____

_____

_____

_____

_____

_____

_____

_____

_____

_____

_____

"I CANNOT THINK OF ANY NEED IN CHILDREN AS STRONG AS THE NEED FOR A FATHER'S PROTECTION." —Sigmund Freud

Did you dress up and go Trick-or-Treating for Halloween when you were young and, if so, what was your favorite costume to wear?

"ONE FATHER IS MORE THAN A HUNDRED SCHOOLMASTERS." —English proverb

What are some of the big, newsworthy events that happened in the world when you were growing up?

What were some of the games your parents played with you outside in the yard or a park?

When do you remember getting into your first fight with another child and what was it about?

"THE CHILDHOOD SHOWS THE MAN, AS MORNING SHOWS THE DAY."
—John Milton

When was the first time you remember doing something that made you feel a sense of pride and what was it?

"WHEN YOU TEACH YOUR SON, YOU TEACH YOUR SON'S SON." —The Talmu

What happened when you got in trouble at home, how were you punished?

What is something you got away with as a child that your parents never found out about?

What did you enjoy most about going to elementary school?

"HOW PLEASANT IT IS FOR A FATHER TO SIT AT HIS CHILD'S BOARD. IT IS LIKE
AN AGED MAN RECLINING UNDER THE SHADOW OF AN OAK WHICH HE HAS
PLANTED." —Walter Scott

What was your favorite thing to eat as a snack after school?

"GENIUS IS NOTHING MORE NOR LESS THAN CHILDHOOD RECAPTURED AT WILL." —Charles Baudelaire

Describe the best present you ever received for your birthday.
What birthday was it?

Tell me about when you first learned to ride a bicycle, skateboard, or scooter.

List five colors that you strongly remember from your childhood and what objects you associate with those colors.

What were you most afraid of when you were little and why?

_____

_____

_____

_____

_____

_____

_____

_____

_____

_____

_____

_____

_____

_____

_____

_____

_____

_____

_____

_____

_____

_____

_____

_____

_____

_____

_____

"SOME GOOD, SACRED MEMORY, PRESERVED FROM CHILDHOOD, IS PERHAPS THE BEST EDUCATION." —Fyodor Dostoyevsky

What was your favorite sweet treat to eat and when were you allowed
to have it?

What do you miss the most about being a child?

"A FATHER IS SOMEONE YOU LOOK UP TO NO MATTER HOW TALL
YOU GROW." —Unknown

CHAPTER III

TEENAGE YEARS

Shouts and laughter as you leave school on a Friday
afternoon, the mischievous smiles of your friends, the
buttery saltiness of popcorn at the movie theater.

"A FATHER IS A BANKER PROVIDED BY NATURE."
—French proverb

Tell me about the first person on whom you had a crush.

"THE GREATEST THING A FATHER CAN DO FOR HIS CHILDREN IS
TO LOVE THEIR MOTHER." —Unknown

When you were in high school, what did you dream of becoming?

Did you play sports in high school and, if so, which ones did you enjoy playing the most?

How would your parents describe you as a teenager?

"AN ANGRY FATHER IS MOST CRUEL TOWARDS HIMSELF." —Publilius Syrus

Were you a rebellious teenager and how frequently did you get in trouble?

"NEVER COULD I EXPECT TO BE SO TRULY BELOVED AND IMPORTANT;
SO ALWAYS FIRST AND ALWAYS RIGHT IN ANY MAN'S EYES AS I
AM IN MY FATHER'S." —Jane Austen

What did you do after school on most days?

Tell me about the teacher who made the biggest impact on you.

What type of music did you like to listen to and what were some of your favorite bands?

"JEKYLL HAD MORE THAN A FATHER'S INTEREST; HYDE HAD MORE THAN A SON'S INDIFFERENCE." —Robert Louis Stevenson

Rank your favorite subjects in school starting with the one you liked best to the one you liked least, and explain why the last subject on the list was your least favorite.

"THE WISEST MAN MAY BE A BLIND FATHER." —Jules Verne

What songs would be on the soundtrack of your high school experience?

How would your high school partner describe your relationship?

Did you go to prom and, if so, who did you take and what was the theme? If not, why not?

_____

_____

_____

_____

_____

_____

_____

_____

_____

_____

_____

_____

_____

_____

_____

_____

_____

_____

_____

_____

_____

_____

_____

_____

"MY FATHER TAUGHT ME TO WORK, BUT NOT TO LOVE IT. I NEVER DID LIKE TO WORK, AND I DON'T DENY IT. I'D RATHER READ, TELL STORIES, CRACK JOKES, TALK, LAUGH—ANYTHING BUT WORK." —Abraham Lincoln

Who taught you how to drive and when did you get your license?

Tell me about the very first car you remember driving alone using all five senses—describe the look, sound, and smell of it and how you felt when you drove it.

When and where did you learn how to swim and who taught you?

Describe your favorite place to go when you needed time alone.

_____

_____

_____

_____

_____

_____

_____

_____

_____

_____

_____

_____

_____

_____

_____

_____

_____

_____

_____

_____

_____

_____

_____

_____

_____

_____

_____

_____

"LISTEN, MY SON, TO YOUR FATHER'S INSTRUCTION AND DO NOT FORSAKE YOUR
MOTHER'S TEACHING." —Proverbs 1:8

What does it say about you in your senior yearbook?

"NO MAN SHOULD BRING CHILDREN INTO THE WORLD WHO IS UNWILLING TO
PERSEVERE TO THE END IN THEIR NATURE AND EDUCATION." —Plato

What extracurricular activities did you participate in at school and which ones were your favorites?

What was your favorite soda pop to drink as a teenager? What other junk food did you like?

Describe your bedroom. What posters and other things did you hang on the walls?

Where in your room did you hide things you did not want your parents to find and what did you hide?

_____

_____

_____

_____

_____

_____

_____

_____

_____

_____

_____

_____

_____

_____

_____

_____

_____

_____

_____

_____

_____

_____

_____

_____

"TOO MANY PARENTS MAKE LIFE HARD FOR THEIR CHILDREN BY TRYING, TOO ZEALOUSLY, TO MAKE IT EASY FOR THEM." —Johann Wolfgang von Goethe

If a movie was made about your high school experience, what actor would play you as a teenager and why?

What is your most embarrassing moment you remember from high school and how long did it affect you?

What are some of the chores you were expected to do around the house when you were growing up and did you receive an allowance?

_____

_____

_____

_____

_____

_____

_____

_____

_____

_____

_____

_____

_____

_____

_____

_____

_____

_____

_____

_____

_____

_____

_____

_____

_____

_____

"LET PARENTS BEQUEATH TO THEIR CHILDREN NOT RICHES, BUT THE
SPIRIT OF REVERENCE." —Plato

What did you do as a teenager to vent whenever you felt frustrated
and angry?

_____

_____

_____

_____

_____

_____

_____

_____

_____

_____

_____

_____

_____

_____

_____

_____

_____

_____

_____

_____

_____

"MY MOTHER DOES NOT CARE FOR THOUGHT, AND FATHER, TOO BUSY
WITH HIS BRIEFS TO NOTICE WHAT WE DO. HE BUYS ME MANY BOOKS,
BUT BEGS ME NOT TO READ THEM, BECAUSE HE FEARS THEY JOGGLE
THE MIND." —Emily Dickinson

How would your best friends in high school describe you?

Are there any people you were friends with in high school that you are still close to now and, if yes, who are they?

If you could go back in time and repeat high school, would you and, if yes, what (if anything) would do differently?

_____
_____
_____
_____
_____
_____
_____
_____
_____
_____
_____
_____
_____
_____
_____
_____
_____
_____
_____
_____
_____
_____
_____
_____
_____
_____

"A MAN'S CHILDREN AND HIS GARDEN BOTH REFLECT THE AMOUNT OF WEEDING DONE DURING THE GROWING SEASON." —Unknown

What was your high school mascot and can you describe what it looked like?

"HE LOVED HIS DAUGHTER BETTER EVEN THAN HIS PIPE, AND, LIKE A
REASONABLE MAN AND AN EXCELLENT FATHER, LET HER HAVE
HER WAY IN EVERYTHING." —Washington Irving

Did you graduate high school and, if so, what do you remember about your graduation day? If you didn't graduate, why not?

What is something you felt misunderstood about when you were a teenager?

What were three goals you remember having in high school and did you achieve them?

_____

_____

_____

_____

_____

_____

_____

_____

_____

_____

_____

_____

_____

_____

_____

_____

_____

_____

_____

_____

_____

_____

_____

_____

_____

_____

_____

_____

_____

"ALACK, WHAT HEINOUS SIN IS IT IN ME, TO BE ASHAM'D TO BE MY FATHER'S CHILD!" —William Shakespeare

What is the wildest party you remember attending in high school and what happened during and afterwards?

"WHAT IS REALLY BEST FOR US LIES ALWAYS WITHIN OUR REACH, THOUGH OFTEN OVERLOOKED." —Henry Wadsworth Longfellow

Describe the hairstyles you wore most often when you were a teenager.

Describe a memory you have of a perfect summer day when you were a teenager.

What was an experience you had as a teenager that really scared you?

"SOME MEMORIES ARE REALITIES AND ARE BETTER THAN ANYTHING THAT CAN
EVER HAPPEN TO ONE AGAIN." —Willa Cather

List five smells that you associate with being a teenager.

"WHAT TIME CAN BE MORE BEAUTIFUL THAN THE ONE IN WHICH THE FINEST
VIRTUES, INNOCENT CHEERFULNESS AND INDEFINABLE LONGING FOR LOVE
CONSTITUTE THE SOLE MOTIVES OF YOUR LIFE?" —Leo Tolstoy

What did you dislike the most about yourself when you were a teenager?

What skill or ability did you feel the most confident about when you were a teenager?

What do you miss most about being a teenager?

"YOUTH IS BUT THE PAINTED SHELL WITHIN WHICH, CONTINUALLY GROWING, LIVES THAT WONDROUS THING THE SPIRIT OF A MAN, BIDING ITS MOMENT OF APPARITION, EARLIER IN SOME THAN IN OTHERS." —Lew Wallace

CHAPTER IV

YOUNG ADULTHOOD

The faded walls of your first apartment, the texture of your favorite pair of jeans, the thrill of exploring unfamiliar destinations in the company of good friends.

"WHEN I WAS A BOY OF FOURTEEN, MY FATHER WAS SO IGNORANT I COULD HARDLY STAND TO HAVE THE OLD MAN AROUND. BUT WHEN I GOT TO BE TWENTY-ONE, I WAS ASTONISHED AT HOW MUCH HE HAD LEARNED IN SEVEN YEARS." —Mark Twain

Did you go to college or trade school and, if so, where and did you finish?

Tell me about the first job you had once you got out of high school.

_____

_____

_____

_____

_____

_____

_____

_____

_____

_____

_____

_____

_____

_____

_____

_____

_____

_____

_____

_____

_____

_____

_____

_____

_____

"THE PATRIOT BLOOD OF MY FATHER WAS WARM IN MY VEINS." —Clara Barton

How would your first boss describe you as a worker?

_____

_____

_____

_____

_____

_____

_____

_____

_____

_____

_____

_____

_____

_____

_____

_____

_____

_____

_____

_____

_____

_____

_____

"MY FATHER SAYS THAT THERE IS ONLY ONE PERFECT VIEW—THE VIEW OF THE SKY STRAIGHT OVER OUR HEADS, AND THAT ALL THESE VIEWS ON EARTH ARE BUT BUNGLED COPIES OF IT." —E. M. Forster

Where was your favorite place to take someone on a first date and why?

At what age did you move out of your parents' house and why?

After leaving your parents' house, did you ever live alone or did you always live with someone else like a roommate or a spouse?

"THE FATHER WHO DOES NOT TEACH HIS SON HIS DUTIES IS EQUALLY GUILTY WITH THE SON WHO NEGLECTS THEM." —Confucius

Did you ever consider joining the military and, if so, what branch appealed to you the most and why?

What clothes did you wear as a young adult that made you feel invincible?

Was there a signature accessory or piece of clothing that you were rarely seen without like a hat or a pair of sunglasses and, if so, describe that item in as much detail as possible.

What are some things you remember as seeming really important to you when you were a young adult?

Were you or any of your friends ever in the hospital?
If yes, why?

_____

"CERTAIN IT IS THAT THERE IS NO KIND OF AFFECTION SO PURELY ANGELIC AS
THAT OF A FATHER TO A DAUGHTER. IN LOVE TO OUR WIVES THERE IS DESIRE; TO
OUR SONS, AMBITION; BUT TO OUR DAUGHTERS THERE IS SOMETHING WHICH
THERE ARE NO WORDS TO EXPRESS." —Joseph Addison

Have you ever had any broken bones and, if so, how did you break them?

What is a huge risk that you took as a young adult, either personally or professionally, that paid off?

Name five people who were hugely important or influential to you during this period of your life and what was your relationship to them.

_____

_____

_____

_____

_____

_____

_____

_____

_____

_____

_____

_____

_____

_____

_____

_____

_____

_____

_____

_____

_____

_____

_____

_____

_____

_____

_____

_____

"O, THAT OUR FATHERS WOULD APPLAUSE OUR LOVES, TO SEAL OUR HAPPINESS
WITH THEIR CONSENTS!" —William Shakespeare

What are the three meals that you cooked for yourself most often when you were a young adult?

What is something that you felt very strongly about when you were
in your twenties?

What was your biggest accomplishment from this period of your life and how did you celebrate it?

What would someone's first impression of you be had they met you at a party when you were in your early twenties?

What were your favorite alcoholic beverages to drink during this period of your life?

_____

_____

_____

_____

_____

_____

_____

_____

_____

_____

_____

_____

_____

_____

_____

_____

_____

_____

_____

_____

_____

_____

_____

_____

_____

_____

_____

_____

"WE THINK OUR FATHERS FOOLS, SO WISE WE GROW. OUR WISER SONS, NO
DOUBT WILL THINK US SO." —Alexander Pope

Did you ever save up money to buy something and, if so, what was it you were saving for and were you eventually able to purchase it?

What is the weirdest experience you had during this period of your life
and did it have any lingering effects?

Was there anything that you felt afraid of as a young adult and, if so, what was it and why did it scare you?

_____

_____

_____

_____

_____

_____

_____

_____

_____

_____

_____

_____

_____

_____

_____

_____

_____

_____

_____

_____

_____

_____

_____

_____

"IF YOU CANNOT GET RID OF THE FAMILY SKELETON, YOU MAY AS WELL MAKE IT DANCE." —George Bernard Shaw

Describe the first place—like a dorm room or apartment—that you lived in after leaving your parent's house using all five senses—what were some sights, smells, tastes, and sounds that you can recall from living there?

"DON'T JUDGE EACH DAY BY THE HARVEST THAT YOU REAP BUT BY THE SEEDS THAT YOU PLANT." —Robert Louis Stevenson

When was your first experience with losing a loved one and what happened?

Name something that profoundly altered your attitudes and approach to life.

Who did you hang out with most often and what did you do?

"ONE FATHER IS ENOUGH TO GOVERN ONE HUNDRED SONS, BUT NOT A
HUNDRED SONS, ONE FATHER." —George Herbert

How did you meet people to date and were you confident when it came to asking out someone you liked?

"A MAN TRAVELS THE WORLD OVER IN SEARCH OF WHAT HE NEEDS, AND RETURNS HOME TO FIND IT." —George Moore

Who was your favorite female celebrity and why?

What kind of shoes did you wear most often as a young adult and can you describe your favorite pair?

Tell me about a time when you went out of your way to help a stranger.

"A PERSON OFTEN MEETS HIS DESTINY ON THE ROAD HE TOOK
TO AVOID IT." —Jean de La Fontaine

If you had to pick a spirit animal, what animal would that be and why?

"FULL WISE IS HE THAT CAN HIMSELF KNOW." —Chaucer

What are five goals that you set for yourself at this time in your life and did you achieve them?

What assumptions would people tend to make about you that
were incorrect?

Who would you describe as your mentor, either professionally or personally and how did they mentor you?

"AS I GROW OLDER, I PAY LESS ATTENTION TO WHAT MEN SAY. I JUST WATCH WHAT THEY DO." —Andrew Carnegie

What celebrity would you swap lives with if you had the chance and why?

"WHY, 'TIS A HAPPY THING TO BE THE FATHER UNTO
MANY SONS." —William Shakespeare

What is something that came easy to you as a young adult?

Did you feel a strong sense of purpose and direction at this point in your life or did you feel like you were struggling to find your way?

Is there anyone that you hung around with that was a bad influence on you and what types of things would you do with them that you didn't do with your other friends?

Did you ever get arrested and, if yes, what for?

"THE BEST INHERITANCE THAT A FATHER CAN LEAVE TO HIS CHILDREN IS THE GLORY
OF HIS VIRTUE AND NOBLE DEEDS." —Cicero

Did you ever participate in a protest and, if yes, for what cause?

CHAPTER V

ADULTHOOD

The scent of your spouse's hair on your wedding day,
the carefree giggle of your first born, your favorite
meal on the dinner table at the end of a long week.

"IT IS A WISE FATHER THAT KNOWS HIS OWN CHILD."
—William Shakespeare

What hobbies do you most like to indulge in as a break from your daily responsibilities?

_____

_____

_____

_____

_____

_____

_____

_____

_____

_____

_____

_____

_____

_____

_____

_____

_____

_____

_____

_____

_____

_____

_____

"WE NEVER KNOW THE LOVE OF A PARENT UNTIL WE BECOME PARENTS OURSELVES." —Henry Ward Beecher

Where is your favorite place to go on vacation with your family?

How did you meet your partner and how long did you date before
you knew they were "the one"?

Which sports do you enjoy watching the most and what is your favorite sporting event to attend in person?

"BLESSED INDEED IS THE MAN WHO HEARS MANY GENTLE VOICES CALL HIM FATHER." —Lydia Maria Child

What age were you when you bought your first couch and
what did it look like?

"YOU HAVE BEEN SO CAREFUL OF ME THAT I NEVER HAD A CHILD'S HEART. YOU
HAVE TRAINED ME SO WELL THAT I NEVER DREAMED A CHILD'S DREAM. YOU HAVE
DEALT SO WISELY WITH ME, FATHER, FROM MY CRADLE TO THIS HOUR, THAT I
NEVER HAD A CHILD'S BELIEF OR A CHILD'S FEAR." —Charles Dickens

Describe what happened when you first learned that you were going to be a father.

What is something you are passionate about that you wish you had more time for?

If you won a million dollars in the lottery, what is the very first thing you would buy and why?

_____

_____

_____

_____

_____

_____

_____

_____

_____

_____

_____

_____

_____

_____

_____

_____

_____

_____

_____

_____

_____

_____

_____

_____

_____

_____

_____

_____

"MOMENTS OF THEIR SECRET LIFE TOGETHER BURST LIKE STARS
UPON HIS MEMORY." —James Joyce

If you had the opportunity to go back to school as an adult, what would you study and why?

_____

_____

_____

_____

_____

_____

_____

_____

_____

_____

_____

_____

_____

_____

_____

_____

_____

_____

_____

_____

_____

_____

_____

_____

"LOVE AND FEAR. EVERYTHING THE FATHER OF A FAMILY SAYS MUST INSPIRE ONE OR THE OTHER." —Joseph Joubert

What is a secret skill you have that most people don't know you have?

What song was playing at your wedding reception when you had your first dance with your spouse after being married? What are some other songs you remember from your wedding day?

What are some things you and your partner liked to do together before you had children?

_____

_____

_____

_____

_____

_____

_____

_____

_____

_____

_____

_____

_____

_____

_____

_____

_____

_____

_____

_____

_____

_____

_____

"NO MAN CAN POSSIBLY KNOW WHAT LIFE MEANS, WHAT THE WORLD MEANS,
WHAT ANYTHING MEANS, UNTIL HE HAS A CHILD A
ND LOVES IT." —Lafcadio Hearn

How involved were you in naming your children and were there any names you liked that your partner was unwilling to consider?

"BEFORE I GOT MARRIED I HAD SIX THEORIES ABOUT RAISING CHILDREN; NOW, I HAVE SIX CHILDREN AND NO THEORIES." —John Wilmo

What are some of the bands you like to listen to as an adult that you could not have imagined liking as a teenager?

What is one thing you told yourself as a young adult you'd never do that you find yourself doing as an adult?

If you could give your mother one big, special gift and money was no object, what would it be and why?

_____

_____

_____

_____

_____

_____

_____

_____

_____

_____

_____

_____

_____

_____

_____

_____

_____

_____

_____

_____

_____

_____

_____

_____

_____

"TO A FATHER GROWING OLD, NOTHING IS DEARER THAN
A DAUGHTER." —Euripides

What languages do you know how to speak and which ones do you wish you knew how to speak?

"MY FATHER'S WIT, AND MY MOTHER'S TONGUE,
ASSIST ME!" —William Shakespeare

Who is someone, either a family member or a friend, do you wish you were able to spend more time with?

Describe in detail your ideal weekend.

What is your fantasy retirement scenario?

"A TRULY RICH MAN IS ONE WHOSE CHILDREN RUN INTO HIS ARMS WHEN HIS
HANDS ARE EMPTY." —Anonymous

Who is someone that had a significant impact on your life that may not realize it and how did they influence you?

_____

_____

_____

_____

_____

_____

_____

_____

_____

_____

_____

_____

_____

_____

_____

_____

_____

_____

_____

_____

_____

_____

_____

"TO UNDERSTAND YOUR PARENTS' LOVE, YOU MUST
RAISE CHILDREN YOURSELF." —Chinese proverb

What is your favorite thing to cook on the grill?

Is the work you do to earn a living as an adult anything like the work you imagined yourself doing when you were younger and, if not, how does it differ?

Who are three of your heroes and why do you admire them?

"CHILDREN ARE A POOR MAN'S WEALTH." —Danish proverb

How do you view the world differently after becoming a father?

"GOVERN A FAMILY AS YOU WOULD COOK A SMALL
FISH—VERY GENTLY." —Chinese Proverb

CHAPTER VI

WISDOM

The quiet pride in a life being lived well, the confidence earned from experience, the joyous hope for the future.

"HE WHO IS TAUGHT TO LIVE UPON LITTLE OWES MORE TO HIS FATHER'S WISDOM THAN HE WHO HAS A GREAT DEAL LEFT HIM DOES TO HIS FATHER'S CARE." —William Penn

What advice would you give your ten-year-old self?

If you could have one do-over, what would it be and why?

_____

_____

_____

_____

_____

_____

_____

_____

_____

_____

_____

_____

_____

_____

_____

_____

_____

_____

_____

_____

_____

_____

_____

_____

_____

_____

_____

_____

"NO MAN HAS EVER LIVED THAT HAD ENOUGH OF CHILDREN'S GRATITUDE OR WOMAN'S LOVE." —William Butler Yeats

What would you say is your worst habit and what would your partner say is your worst habit?

Have you ever won anything and, if so, what was it?

Who is the most famous person you've ever met and how did you chance upon meeting them?

What do you consider to be the proudest moment of your life so far?

"REPUTATION IS WHAT MEN AND WOMEN THINK OF US, CHARACTER IS WHAT
GOD AND THE ANGELS KNOW OF US." —Thomas Paine

What is the best piece of advice you were ever given and who gave it to you?

"HIS LIFE WAS GENTLE; AND THE ELEMENTS SO MIX'D IN HIM, THAT NATURE MIGHT
STAND UP, AND SAY TO ALL THE WORLD, 'THIS WAS A MAN!'"
—William Shakespeare

What are five questions you wish you could ask your own father?

Is there something you've done in your past that you still feel ashamed about and, if so, what is it?

List the five happiest days of your life so far and what happened on those days to make them so special.

_____

"THE OLDER I GET, THE MORE CLEARLY I REMEMBER THINGS THAT NEVER HAPPENED." —Mark Twain

Where in the world would you travel if money and time were no object?

"KNOWLEDGE COMES, BUT WISDOM LINGERS." —Alfred Tennyson

What celebrity would you most like to have lunch with, living or dead, and what are five questions you would ask them?

What advice would you give your twenty-year-old-self?

If you could apologize face-to-face to any one person in your past that you have wronged, who would it be and what happened that makes you feel the need to apologize?

"NOTHING FIXES A THING SO INTENSELY IN THE MEMORY AS THE WISH TO FORGET IT." —Michel de Montaigne

What is your most prized possession?

"WHEN YOU ARISE IN THE MORNING, THINK OF WHAT A PRECIOUS PRIVILEGE IT IS
TO BE ALIVE—TO BREATHE, TO THINK, TO ENJOY, TO LOVE." —Marcus Aurelius

What is one thing, an object such as a book, souvenir, or piece of clothing, that you recall from your past that you no longer have but wish you did?

Were you ever seriously ill and, if so, from what and how did recovering change your outlook on life?

List five of your favorite books and who wrote them.

"I SAT IN THE SUN ON A BENCH; THE ANIMAL WITHIN ME LICKING THE
CHOPS OF MEMORY." —Robert Louis Stevenson

List five of your favorite movies and explain why each one had an impact on you.

List five things that you think every person should experience at some point during their life and why.

Tell me one secret you have that nobody else knows.

How do you want people to remember you, is there one particular
accomplishment that you hope will define your legacy?

"IF YOU TELL THE TRUTH, YOU DON'T HAVE TO REMEMBER ANYTHING."
—Mark Twain

What is your favorite meal to indulge in when you are treating yourself or celebrating something?

_____

_____

_____

_____

_____

_____

_____

_____

_____

_____

_____

_____

_____

_____

_____

_____

_____

_____

_____

_____

_____

_____

_____

_____

_____

"I PRESSED MY FATHER'S HAND AND TOLD HIM I WOULD PROTECT HIS GRAVE WITH
MY LIFE. MY FATHER SMILED AND PASSED AWAY TO THE SPIRIT LAND."
—Chief Joseph

What is something from your childhood that is no longer available that you wish you could experience now?

What advice would you give your thirty-year-old-self?

If you could have any super power, what would it be, why, and how would you use it for the very first time?

What is something that you always wanted to learn but haven't yet?

"REMEMBRANCE OF THINGS PAST IS NOT NECESSARILY THE REMEMBRANCE OF
THINGS AS THEY WERE." —Marcel Proust

If you could have front row tickets to see any band or musician, living or dead, who would it be?

What is something different about the world now that you never imagined when you were younger?

What is something you learned about yourself as a result of becoming a father?

_____

_____

_____

_____

_____

_____

_____

_____

_____

_____

_____

_____

_____

_____

_____

_____

_____

_____

_____

_____

_____

_____

_____

_____

_____

_____

_____

"IN FAMILY LIFE, LOVE IS THE OIL THAT EASES FRICTION, THE CEMENT THAT BINDS
CLOSER TOGETHER, AND THE MUSIC THAT BRINGS HARMONY."
—Friedrich Nietzsche

If you could change one thing about the world today, what would it be?

"MEMORY IS THE DIARY THAT CHRONICLES THINGS THAT NEVER HAPPENED OR COULDN'T POSSIBLY HAVE HAPPENED." —Oscar Wilde

What is something you hope to accomplish that you haven't yet?

What is something you secretly like that would surprise the people who know you well?

Who do you consider to be your best friend right now?

_____

_____

_____

_____

_____

_____

_____

_____

_____

_____

_____

_____

_____

_____

_____

_____

_____

_____

_____

_____

_____

_____

_____

_____

_____

"TIME IS THE FATHER OF TRUTH, ITS MOTHER IS OUR MIND." —Giordano Bruno

Brimming with creative inspiration, how-to projects, and useful information to enrich your everyday life, Quarto Knows is a favorite destination for those pursuing their interests and passions. Visit our site and dig deeper with our books into your area of interest: Quarto Creates, Quarto Cooks, Quarto Homes, Quarto Lives, Quarto Drives, Quarto Explores, Quarto Gifts, or Quarto Kids.

© 2020 BY QUARTO PUBLISHING GROUP USA INC.

FIRST PUBLISHED IN 2020 BY CHARTWELL BOOKS, AN IMPRINT OF THE QUARTO GROUP, 142 WEST 36TH STREET, 4TH FLOOR, NEW YORK, NY 10018, USA T (212) 779-4972 F (212) 779-6058 WWW.QUARTOKNOWS.COM

CHARTWELL TITLES ARE ALSO AVAILABLE AT DISCOUNT FOR RETAIL, WHOLESALE, PROMOTIONAL, AND BULK PURCHASE. FOR DETAILS, CONTACT THE SPECIAL SALES MANAGER BY EMAIL AT SPECIALSALES@QUARTO.COM OR BY MAIL AT THE QUARTO GROUP, ATTN: SPECIAL SALES MANAGER, 100 CUMMINGS CENTER SUITE 265D, BEVERLY, MA 01915 USA.

10 9 8 7 6 5 4 3 2

ISBN: 978-0-7858-3910-1

PUBLISHER: RAGE KINDELSPERGER
CREATIVE DIRECTOR: LAURA DREW
MANAGING EDITOR: CARA DONALDSON
TEXT: CHRISTOPHER O'BRIEN
COVER DESIGN AND INTERIOR DESIGN: BETH MIDDLEWORTH

PRINTED IN CHINA TT012021